GRAPHIC
SCIENCE

MAX AXIOM AND THE SOCIETY OF SUPER SCIENTISTS

RAINFOREST DESTRUCTION

WRITTEN BY **CAROL KIM**
ILLUSTRATED BY **EDUARDO GARCIA**
COVER BY **ERIK DOESCHER**

Raintree is an imprint of Capstone Global Library Limited, a company
incorporated in England and Wales having its registered office at 264
Banbury Road, Oxford, OX2 7DY – Registered company number:
6695582

www.raintree.co.uk
myorders@raintree.co.uk

Edited by Abby Huff and Aaron Sautter
Designed by Brann Garvey
Media researched by Svetlana Zhurkin
Original illustrations © Capstone Global Library Limited 2022
Cover Art by Erik Doescher
Production by Kathy McColley
Originated by Capstone Global Library Ltd
Printed and bound in India

978 1 3982 3390 4

British Library Cataloguing in Publication Data
A full catalogue record for this book is available from the British
Library.

CONTENTS

THE SOCIETY OF SUPER SCIENTISTS

MAX AXIOM

After years of study, Max Axiom, the world's first Super Scientist, knew the mysteries of the universe were too vast for one person alone to uncover. So Max created the Society of Super Scientists! Using their superpowers and super-brains, this talented group investigates today's most urgent scientific and environmental issues and learns about actions everyone can take to solve them.

LIZZY AXIOM

NICK AXIOM

SPARK

THE DISCOVERY LAB

Home of the Society of Super Scientists, this state-of-the-art lab houses advanced tools for cutting-edge research and radical scientific innovation. More importantly, it is a space for Super Scientists to collaborate and share knowledge as they work together to tackle any challenge.

The Super Scientists' tree planting project at the Discovery Lab is about to grow into an urgent environmental mission to help the world's rainforests.

One day this tree will provide some nice shade and help clean the air.

Thanks for your help with digging, Spark!

Good thing you've been working on your planting skills. I've just had a call from Brazil. A group needs help with a reforestation project.

They need help planting trees? We can do that!

These aren't just any trees. The group is working to restore the rainforests.

That's an important project. Rainforests are being destroyed all the time. More than half of Earth's rainforests have been lost already.

Then we don't have any time to lose. Let's go!

> Rainforests are found all over the world. The one we're heading to is the Amazon forest in South America.

> Tropical rainforests are found near the equator. They stay warm all year long. Temperatures range from 20 to 35 degrees Celsius or 68 to 95 degrees Fahrenheit.

> It rains almost every day in these woody areas. Anywhere from 150 to 1,020 centimetres, or 60 to 400 inches of rainfall each year!

RAINFORESTS AT THE SOUTH POLE?

Rainforests are currently found on every continent on Earth, except for Antarctica. But due to a recent discovery, the South Pole no longer has to be left out - at least if you count rainforests that existed 90 million years ago! Scientists drilling deep in the ground in West Antarctica discovered traces of an ancient forest. Plant remains in soil samples show the area was once home to a temperate rainforest, which has cooler temperatures than a tropical forest.

Hello, Rodrigo!

Welcome to Brazil, Super Scientists! Thank you for coming. Our rainforests need help!

We're ready to learn more.

Earth's largest rainforest is the Amazon. It covers almost 40 per cent of South America.

But since 1978, about 1 million square kilometres, or 386,000 square miles, has been destroyed. That's an area almost the size of Egypt!

And the Amazon isn't the only place in trouble.

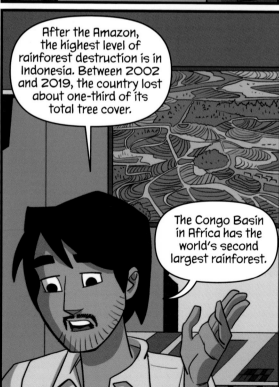

After the Amazon, the highest level of rainforest destruction is in Indonesia. Between 2002 and 2019, the country lost about one-third of its total tree cover.

The Congo Basin in Africa has the world's second largest rainforest.

From 2000 to 2014, it lost about 160,000 square kilometres, or 61,700 square miles, of forest. That's more than twice the size of Ireland.

The rate of loss is increasing quickly. Some researchers believe we could lose all rainforests within the next 100 years!

How can we help?

Our tree planting programme works to restore forests in Brazil. But we also need to educate others about rainforest destruction, so we can all take action to stop it.

I can stay to help plant trees.

And Lizzy and I can do more research into the rainforest crisis.

Fantástico!

It's clear Earth's rainforests are in trouble. But why are we losing them?

Unfortunately, human activity is a big reason.

Many rainforests are destroyed when people cut down the trees to clear the land. This is called deforestation.

Farmers often take another step. They burn what's left of the trees in a process called slash and burn.

They burn it? Why?

Rainforest soil isn't very good for farming. The ash from burned trees puts nutrients into the soil that help plants grow.

But after about two years, the nutrients are used up. So the farmers move on. They cut down and burn more forest.

Cleared land is often made into pastures. In the Amazon and Central America, more than 70 per cent of deforestation is due to cattle ranching.

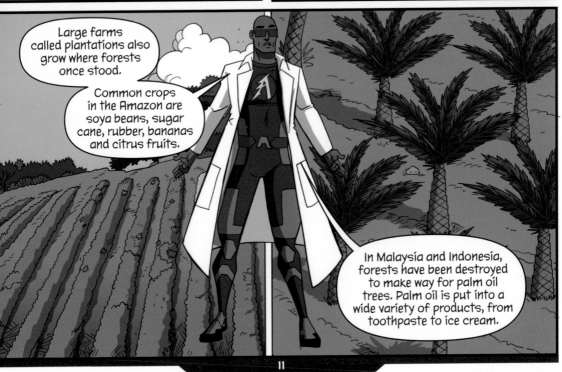

Large farms called plantations also grow where forests once stood.

Common crops in the Amazon are soya beans, sugar cane, rubber, bananas and citrus fruits.

In Malaysia and Indonesia, forests have been destroyed to make way for palm oil trees. Palm oil is put into a wide variety of products, from toothpaste to ice cream.

In the Amazon, around 95 per cent of deforestation takes place within 50 kilometres, or 30 miles, of a road.

Mining is another issue, particularly in the Congo and Amazon. To remove minerals such as gold from the soil, miners use mercury.

That chemical is highly toxic. It strips the soil of nutrients.

Right, and that makes mining especially destructive. Over time, rainforest plants can regrow on old farmland. But land that has been mined may be ruined permanently.

Other governments decide not to make it a priority. For example, Brazil focused on rainforest protections in the early 2000s. Amazon destruction fell by 80 per cent over eight years.

But in 2016 and 2018, policies changed. The government cut budgets for its environmental protection programmes.

By 2019, Brazil reached its highest deforestation rate in over a decade. So much of the Amazon was burning that the smoke could be seen from space.

These incredible places are in danger of disappearing, and it's important to understand what we risk losing along with the forests.

Let's have a look.

Many living things are put in danger when rainforests are destroyed. They're home to about 60 per cent of all land life on Earth.

As their habitats are wiped out, animals may be lost forever.

An incredible variety of plants grow here too. Some are even used in medicines. In fact, 70 per cent of plants used in cancer treatments are found only in rainforests.

If the rainforest disappears, undiscovered cures could also be lost forever.

TOO MANY TO COUNT

Rainforests are home to an amazing variety of species. No one knows exactly how many. Estimates range from 3 to 50 million, and the numbers are still rising. For example, a two-year study by the World Wildlife Fund in the Amazon region discovered an average of one new species every two days. But with the high rate of tropical deforestation, scientists fear some species may become extinct before we even have a chance to discover them.

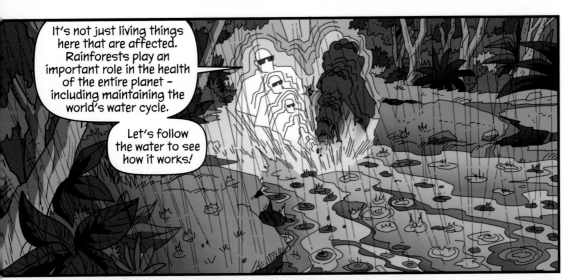

It's not just living things here that are affected. Rainforests play an important role in the health of the entire planet – including maintaining the world's water cycle.

Let's follow the water to see how it works!

The trees pull water from the ground with their roots . . .

. . . and later release the water through their leaves as vapour into the air.

The water vapour forms clouds. Some of the clouds travel across the globe, bringing moisture to other parts of the world.

It's like we're in a river in the sky!

When enough water collects in the clouds, it falls back down as rain.

But the loss of rainforests is upsetting this process. Fewer trees mean less water vapour is released into the sky. That leads to less rain, which leads to more droughts.

Rainforests have another big role in the planet's health. In order to live, trees "breathe in" carbon dioxide, or CO2. Rainforest trees absorb billions of tonnes of carbon from the gas each year.

We need to start taking action. How can we stop using the land in ways that harm the environment?

It's a challenging problem. People who live near rainforests are often poor. They clear the trees because they don't have other ways to provide for their families.

But it is possible to live on rainforest land without destroying it. Mercedes here of the Kichwa tribe can tell us more.

That's right!

Just take a look at the two sides on this road. The forested side is protected tribal lands.

Wow! The difference is like night and day.

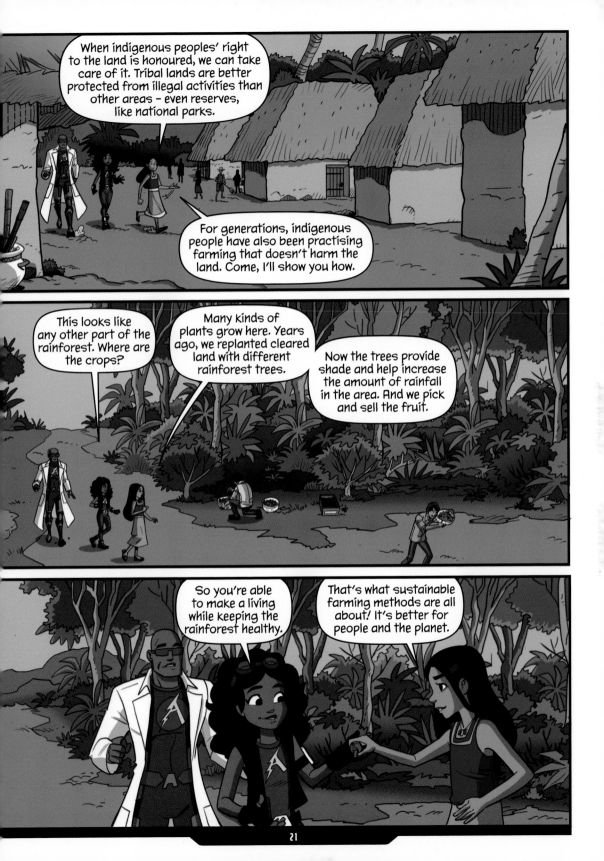

Let's look at another forest-friendly option at work here in Costa Rica. *Hola*, Adilia!

Hola, Max! Welcome to our beautiful *Bosque Eterno de los Niños*, or Children's Eternal Rainforest.

This reserve was created through donations from children all over the world.

People come here to see the rainforests and the wildlife.

Oh! That sloth is so cute!

Tourists who visit areas to see the natural environment, like this rainforest, support something called ecotourism. Ecotourism fights deforestation in a number of ways.

One way is by raising awareness of the issue. Visitors learn about rainforests and why they need to be protected.

If you listen carefully, you may hear the "Bong!" of the three-wattled bell bird.

COSTA RICA
1983

COSTA RICA
2010

Look for products that don't harm rainforests. Organizations such as the Rainforest Alliance certify food and other products that have sustainably grown ingredients.

You can look for their seal.

When we buy these products, we support farmers who are trying to protect and restore the forests.

And of course, another way to help the forests is to plant more trees! Who's ready to get to work?

Me!

I am!

HOW KIDS SAVED A RAINFOREST

The issue of rainforest destruction can sometimes feel too big and too far away to do anything about it. But one group of children believed they should try.

During the 1980s, rainforests were experiencing some of the highest rates of deforestation in history. In 1987, far from the tropics, a group of 9- and 10-year-old schoolchildren in Sweden learned about rainforests. They watched videos of trees being cut down and burned. Upset, the children asked what they could do to help. Finally, one pupil asked, "Why can't we buy some rainforest?"

It seemed like a far-fetched solution – but it was one that could protect some rainforest land. The children were determined to try. The class started holding bake sales and performing plays to raise money. They were delighted to learn that the £170 they raised could be used to purchase about 5 hectares (12 acres) of rainforest for protection in Costa Rica.

Inspired by their success, the class kept working to raise money. A television station broadcast a performance by the class to raise awareness about the rainforests. More money was raised, and more children got involved. The Swedish government gave £57,000 grant towards the purchase of more rainforest. By the end of the year, the children had raised £85,000. But they were just getting started. Word kept spreading, and by 1992, children from 44 countries helped raise £1.4 million.

The money was sent to the Monteverde Conservation League (MCL), an environmental organization in Costa Rica. The MCL used the money to purchase what eventually became more than 22,500 hectares (56,000 acres) of rainforest reserve. To honour the children, the reserve was named the *Bosque Eterno de los Ninos* (BEN), or Children's Eternal Rainforest. It is now the largest private reserve in Costa Rica.

All this because of a group of 9- and 10-year-olds who wanted to protect an important resource that was located on the other side of the world.

GLOSSARY

atmosphere mixture of gases that surrounds a planet

carbon dioxide gas with no colour or smell that plants take in and people and animals breathe out; abbreviated CO2, the gas is also formed by burning fuels or through the breakdown of plant and animal matter

certify officially stating that something has met certain requirements or a quality level

climate average weather of a place over a long period of time

deforestation act or process of cutting down all the trees in an area

ecotourism practice of visiting a natural environment in a way that does not harm the land or wildlife; ecotourism is meant to help support the local economy while also supporting efforts to protect nature

enforce make sure laws or rules are followed

fossil fuel fuel formed in the Earth from the remains of plants and animals; coal, oil and natural gas are fossil fuels

indigenous of or relating to the people who are the original, earliest known inhabitants of a region

petition letter signed by many people asking leaders or a group for a change

reserve area where the land and wildlife are protected

sapling young tree

sustainable done in a way that can be continued without destroying or completely using up natural resources

FIND OUT MORE

Can You Save a Tropical Rainforest? (You Choose: Eco Expeditions), Eric Braun (Raintree, 2021)

Endangered Rainforests (Endangered Earth), Rani Iyer (Raintree, 2020)

Rainforests (Flowchart Science: Habitats and Ecosystems), Louise & Richard Spilsbury (Raintree, 2020)

WEBSITES

www.bbc.co.uk/bitesize/clips/zfp34wx
Find out about threats to the rainforest from businesses and farming with this BBC Bitesize video clip.

www.dkfindout.com/uk/animals-and-nature/habitats-and-ecosystems/amazon-rainforest/
Learn more about the Amazon Rainforest at the DK Findout! website.

INDEX